The poems in this collection are alive with humor and heartbreak, fear and narcotic discomfort. Deep weirdness. Psychosexual monologues. They are intimate and contemporary. Impeccably crafted. Deceptive in their simplicity. They read like they were written five minutes ago and then whispered into somebody's ear. These are field reports from the edges of Los Angeles, delivered in language that is unusually open, immediate, and clear. Mira Gonzalez must have really good eyesight, I think.
– Brad Listi, host of the Otherppl Podcast.

What distinguishes the poems in Mira Gonzalez's debut collection is her ability to channel a deeply inner world through contemporary imagery, and to do it honestly. These are clever poems that watch themselves, but they do not rest on self-knowledge alone. The watcher goes ever deeper, questioning its own wants, its isolation, as well as intimacies that may not have existed as remembered. Men make promises as to where they will come and then don't. Love renders you "twice as frail as you were before" and resembles cough medicine. Emotions that "light a bank on fire" are held at a distance, but they are very there. These are poems that want to be told that their "physical presence in the world has caused you to experience extreme disequilibrium." They will. Watch this eye.
– Melissa Broder, author of Scarecrone and So Sad Today.

**i will never be beautiful enough
to make us beautiful together**

mira gonzalez

© 2013 mira gonzalez
© 2013 sorry house

cover design by haley stark
formatted by willis plummer
edited by spencer madsen, frank hinton, and omar de col

first edition, third printing

sorry house
sorry.house

for media queries, domestic wholesale information, or
general inquiries, contact:
spencer@sorry.house

distributed in europe by antenne books:
antennebooks.com

isbn: 0988839407
isbn13: 978-0-9888394-0-3

i will never be beautiful enough
to make us beautiful together

mortal kombat

I am thinking about those tiny clams that bury themselves under wet
sand at the beach
I identify with the tiny clams
I want to bury myself under wet sand
my cat is giving me a disapproving look
I pick up my cat and forcibly hug her
my cat meows loudly and jump-kicks me as she runs away
I think I would like to be a cat
I want someone to forcibly hug me
I want to jump-kick them and run away
I begin to count how many people I have had sex with in my life
I say out loud:
'I don't care about the people I've had sex with. I like being alone.
being with other people is tiring'
I am talking to myself
'mira is talking to herself'
I want to take a bath with all the lights off
the couple that lives next door are yelling at each other again
I feel happy that my neighbors have a relationship that is important
enough to yell about

ryan gosling

I am becoming increasingly hostile and unsympathetic
social interaction makes me feel tired and irritated
I have alienated myself
I don't have meaningful relationships
I don't have romantic relationships
I read a lot of depressing books
I like being alone
I am a bland person
I am an afterthought
I am a bag of unsalted pretzels
I don't know
I am constantly reaching towards some nebulous goal
I am not a mean person
I am not a bad person
I am only okay

symbolic interactionism

people walk from one destination to another
with looks of determination on their faces
they stare at me
and they say 'where the fuck are you going'
I say 'I am going to a place'
they say 'fuck you'
and I have an intense feeling of being a pathetic asshole
and that feeling manifests itself in the form of frantic unrestrained
movement

I begin to realize that my face will never be inside of your face
and that we can silently communicate using a series of microscopic
gestures

and we will understand that the phrase 'alone together' is not an
oxymoron anymore

and I will resolve to never be happy enough to forgive you

and I promise that from now on I will only have emotions that can be
perceived as neutral

I wonder how it is possible that there are billions of people in the world
yet I am the only person on the planet

secular humanist

stephen was lying in a large puddle
he was thinking about you being naked
sometimes you are naked in your room, or in your bathroom
he liked the idea of you being naked
stephen felt jealous of you because you get to see yourself naked all
the time
stephen never gets to see you naked
you are probably beautiful and vulnerable when you're naked
he wants to find every bone in your body
all two hundred and six of them
he wants to feel them through your naked skin with his fingertips
he wants to name them as he finds them
'clavicle, manubrium, sternum'
outside, stephen can feel the winter air against his skin
stephen is not naked
stephen is wearing clothes
stephen is lying in a large puddle
stephen grabs a little bit of mud with his hands
stephen touches his glasses and gets mud on the lens
his vision is obscured
he feels like a grain of sand, on a beach, that isn't a real grain of sand,
but is actually a very tiny piece of a clamshell from a clam that died 10
years ago

list of pornographic sub-genres

I was romantically involved with a 29 year old who had a master's degree in philosophy
he took me on a date and bought me dinner
after dinner we kissed and touched each other in the backseat of my car
he said 'I'm gonna come on your stomach' 15 to 20 times while breathing heavily and putting his penis on different parts of my stomach
every time I attempted to touch his penis he moved my hand away
eventually I gave up on trying to interact with his penis

he never came on my stomach
also he was afraid of elevators

**you will roll around in an empty parking lot with him
until you lose circulation in your limbs and forget
your own name (everything is okay)**

we sat in the backseat of your car
which was parked on a tall cliff
overlooking the ocean at 1 am
you described a plot for a movie
loosely based on your life
you were played by james franco
your girlfriend was played by lindsay lohan
during the climax of the movie
james franco ties lindsay lohan to a chair in his house
then he pours gasoline on a pile of money
and lights the money on fire
the house burns down and they both die
the credits roll and you pull me toward you
by the neck of my shirt
your index finger is in my mouth when you say
'we don't have to'

the main purpose of the heart is to make heart sounds

the next time you are driving your car
you will think about that day we had sex in my dad's bed
when the bright sun was shining on us through white curtains
and we felt comforted by the inevitability of death

I know sometimes late at night we share the same thoughts
we think that we only have free will when we are alone
and that we don't want to become better people

the newspaper said that the sun erupted tuesday evening
and that the higgs boson particle created a ripple in the space time
continuum
and that beer is good for you

I will touch your face using my entire body
and we will recall a specific warm morning
when we felt numbness in the space between atoms
and our mouths tasted like the unattainable closeness of years prior

untitled 1

kick me hard in the back of my knees
collapsing on the ground
placid and self-sufficient
specific nostalgic emotions
long necklaces and long hair
sudden acute pain in a mysterious organ
touch parts of my brain with your fingers
physically stimulate certain memories
of christmas eve, three years ago
when I had nobody to tell
a kind of silent cloying apology

untitled 2

I am sitting on the hood of your car
in front of an elementary school in the rain

I am using barely perceptible hand gestures
to describe the feeling I get at night
in the last five minutes before falling asleep
of wanting our molecules to occupy the same space

you are telling the police that I'm your girlfriend
you are putting your cigarette out on the bottom of my shoe
I am not your girlfriend

time passes

you say 'why are you doing this'
I tell you that I don't understand the question
you say 'please don't do this'

the left side of your face is momentarily illuminated by the headlights
of a passing car

at 5:30 in the morning

when the sky has shifted from black to dark blue
we start to have this panicked feeling
that maybe we will never sleep
and when I wear your misshapen cashmere sweater tonight
it will feel like I'm putting my face on you again
in order to perceive a very small thing inside your chest
perhaps we can understand this unique sort of indifference
which is sometimes felt on the rough surface of a refrigerator
and in the weird light behind the skin on your fingers
and in the years which have run you down

I can read a novel out loud while you lie on my floor with your head in my lap and we can feel happy because we are touching each other and I am using my voice and we don't have to think about climate change or death

I drank a bottle of wine and swallowed ambien
I felt preemptive regret about the immediate future
while we had sex on my floor
I made noises with my mouth
and watched cartoons on the TV
I thought 'do porn stars feel sad'
'I feel sad'
I kissed you once and felt self-aware and stopped kissing you
I watched you fall asleep on my bed
I wished you were a specific person
I walked around my house at 4 in the morning
or dreamt about walking around my house at 4 in the morning
my cat expressed disappointment and irritation and other emotions
I noticed foreign details on my naked body in the bathroom mirror
I couldn't feel or move one of my thumbs
I touched my collar bone where a bruise would form the next day
I touched things in my kitchen
coffee grounds, alfalfa sprouts, counter top, short grain brown rice
I imagined the face of a specific person and tried to make myself cry
I imagined wrapping my entire body around this person's leg
I thought about 100 degree weather and factories that manufacture
whole wheat pasta

mcsweeney's caused global warming

lately I have been watching this emotion
cautiously, from a safe distance
today this emotion lit a bank on fire
and developed a cult following
I am going to consume your entire body
by lying down on top of you and breathing very hard
and we will feel alienated by way of osmosis
would you please push your head against my head
until we can mutually confirm our place in the universe
did you know that I can only have an orgasm
when I am lying down on my back
also I have never seen snow
a decrease in the number of microscopic particles
between my mouth and your fingers
has caused me to experience extremely positive feelings
also anxiety and severe depression
I am concentrating on becoming 40mg of adderall right now

I just need you to know exactly what I want without me having to say anything

do you remember that dream I had
where my fingers touched your fingers
and we came to understand that our hands were capable of
expressing complex emotions as separate entities from our bodies
could you just put your mouth on my mouth next time you talk
I have been trained through operant conditioning
to react negatively to romantic emotional stimulus
now I feel comfort because your brain
is encased in a skull a few miles away from here
I'm sorry
saying words that have positive connotations
will cause catastrophic weather patterns
I am severely delusional and I have poor impulse control
it's fine, I'm good
now look at my face and tell me
that my physical presence in the world
has caused you to experience extreme disequilibrium
are you able to confirm my existence
in a strictly biological sense
wait, no
will you just hold on for one second
I have to hide under my bed for two years

self-defeating personality disorder

a few visceral emotions
creating a small and heavy thing
this idea in my stomach
limbs reaching forward and around with platonic willingness
touching your face for an indeterminate amount of time
human density that causes nearby birds
to suffer minor neurological damage
can you feel this permanent concept beneath my ribcage
you cannot create anything or feel something that nobody has felt
before

I wrote a novel about you and saved it to my drafts folder

the effect of certain drugs
is to make you feel crippled in bed at five in the morning
a nondescript emotion
this is how I feel on saturday
my thoughts have the punishing timbre of a small child's voice
sexually active teenagers in the midwest
receiving money and slowly becoming deformed
I used to be this person three hours ago
I am the absence of something sentient
telling people I prefer to be alone
which is true sometimes

I am trying to parallel park my car
I am trying to make you love me

semi-humorous paradox

would you put some coffee grounds on your tongue
and then put your tongue in my hand

in my dream I watched you masturbate
while floating 5 inches above you
I was invisible until I kissed your mouth
will you let me do that tomorrow afternoon
I will text you

when I sneeze multiple times in quick succession
it feels like a tiny orgasm in my face

today I am going to fill my bathtub with milk
and if my nose starts bleeding
the milk will turn pink
then maybe you could lick my face
and tell me that my blood tastes like pennies
why do we both know what pennies taste like

it is june and he wants to leave your room

he is sitting next to you on your bed
pointing at things on your computer screen
typing sentences and deleting them
he walks to your bookshelf
holding a book in each hand
he says 'did you like this book'
you don't know which book he is referring to
his sleeves are an inch too long and he looks cold
you remember a dream you had
you were lying on top of him
touching his mouth with your mouth sometimes
now you are folding your limbs inward
holding them near your chest
you are trying to become very small and round
you want to be quiet and alone with him
for a few hours or a few years

heartbroken people with extreme personality flaws

I want to feel orgasms in the tip of my nose and the back of my ear
in the cartilage between the vertebrae that make up my spinal column
would you stare at my face for two hours without blinking
standing on the splintery wooden porch of the house where I was born
we are craving a certain unachievable density in emotions
subtle gestures that suggest something complex and vague
I will kiss you everywhere and recklessly
under an avocado tree in the hole I dug in my dad's backyard when I
was seven
here are some things that I would like to touch
clavicle bones, backs of knees, adam's apples, the spaces between
fingers
together we will have this extremely beautiful sensation
of being twice as frail as we once were
and it will feel like the first time you ever had a cold
the last time you tasted grape flavored cough syrup
a light pink fever

untitled 3

fish who swim in schools with thousands of other identical fish
perceive themselves as unique and lonely
I have displayed my ability to fit perfectly into a human-shaped box
may I put your face in my face
I have been doing this thing
I have been indiscriminately killing nearby insects
do you love me as a six year old child
displaying this sort of uncontrolled blindness
that is only seen in certain breeds of rodent
the day I met my dad for the first time
a rejected emotion was discovered
I focused on creating this enormous empty space
and discovering the meanings of words based on context
I am on top of you in a bed
I am lying in the fetal position near your head like a cat
it hurt us both when I held you from behind
because I couldn't change the weather with my arms

untitled 4

there was this house I used to see when I was a kid
I believed a witch lived in this house
the witch sat in a wheelchair and stared at people
I would make eye contact with her
and think 'I am going to die eventually'

this was the only house on a gentrified street
with a lot of expensive coffee shops and upscale boutiques

this house had many lawn ornaments

large men wearing wife beaters
with tattoos on their arms
sat on the porch and drank malt liquor

an old woman sometimes screamed at people from a window
she yelled things like
'cock sucking mother fucker'
'lesbian whore'
'CUNT'

I felt genuine affection for this house
it became an empty lot last week

today I walked by it
I saw dead grass and broken ornaments
surrounded by a tall chain-link fence
I felt afraid and indignant that the house didn't exist anymore

I thought 'a house is not sentient'
and felt myself resign to a kind of deficient logical reasoning
that is mostly seen in young children

a woman ran towards me from the other side of the fence
she shouted 'mother fucking lesbian whore'
'fuck you cunt. what the fuck'
I mumbled 'sorry. I'm sorry' as I walked away
I thought 'this is okay'

everything is okay

I will never be beautiful enough to make us beautiful together

if I were two inches tall
I would sit on your shoulder all day
and nurture a relationship with your earlobe
my hands would be too small to effectively touch you
I would create empty space using the tip of my tongue
and feel afraid of every bone in my body
especially my sit bones

palm trees are not native to los angeles

lying on the sidewalk
on venice boulevard

I am able to perceive this
inconceivably large distance
between myself and the street

I am trying to become
two squares of cement

I am one fraction of the pacific ocean
compared to me everything is enormous

I am focusing on empty space
between barely visible sea anemones
which cling to the underside of piers

I felt 3 earthquakes last week

it is going to be 73 degrees today

there are exactly 4 clouds in the sky

I am one unit of matter
moving through time
at this incredible pace

untitled 5

I am looking at people who are dancing and touching each other
I am drinking vodka with ice and feeling incredibly fucked
I wonder if anyone feels more lonely now than they felt an hour ago
when they were alone in their rooms looking at things on the internet

untitled 6

last night you told me
that everything in your life
is a shade of light green
I touched your leg under the table
you spilled wine on my shoe
the next morning we woke up
thirsty and alone in our respective beds
we allowed tenuously beautiful memories
to momentarily occupy our minds

untitled 7

avoid seeing a person who has expressed sexual interest in you
agree to seeing this person and have sex with him in the backseat of
his car
sit on the hood of the car and smoke one of his cigarettes
you don't like the taste of cigarettes and you never smoke them
you see dust mites in a ray of light coming from a streetlamp
and feel panic
you are extremely allergic to dust mites

I will inevitably ruin our relationship

you and I slept on a couch together
we were at a friend's house
I had consumed an indiscernible amount of alcohol
I don't remember you getting on the couch with me
I remember waking up and seeing that someone was next to me
and my head was in the space between his arm and his chest
I felt warm and dizzy
I adjusted my body and realized that it was you
my face was looking up at your face
I wasn't thinking about anything
life was progressing against my perception of time
I had no idea how long I had been asleep
you started kissing me
I had this specific shitty feeling
I closed my eyes and thought about virtual particles
that cease to exist when they are not observed
the momentum of a virtual particle is uncertain according to the
uncertainty principle
it is also uncertain whether or not I existed while I was kissing you
you are my friend and I am not supposed to be kissing you
you said 'do you want to have sex?'
I said 'no' and immediately felt guilty
our mouths were dry and smelled like alcohol
you grabbed me through my soft cotton shirt
we didn't pretend to feel aroused
you grabbing me does not affect the world in any way
in the morning you showed me cuts on your back
and told me that you had blacked out the night before

in the space between our bodies

there is a cup holder filled with pennies
a distance which can often take years to cross
blood on my lips changing the color of yours slightly
as if we came into existence this way
I almost knew what you wanted then
but something happened
you lost both of your shoes that night
you told me everything was still the same
except for a pile of books
and a sliding glass door
and a cup of cold water
you said 'can we just lie here for a bit'
your legs moved in strange patterns across me
i walked down the stairs from your balcony
and into the alley behind your apartment

5 years old

I wake up on a mattress in the living room
I ride a plastic tricycle in circles around the kitchen
until my mom wakes up
I eat cereal next to a window
in blue crayon, I draw a picture
of a woman walking her dog

I have come to understand certain things
that the slide in my backyard causes splinters
and there are dead crickets in the heating vents

he is embracing me
not a hug, not really
he is kneeling and I am standing
we are the same height this way

over his shoulder I can see marble stairs
I feel confused or afraid
he gives me a teddy bear

a year later, he will get married
at the wedding I throw petals down the aisle
wearing a handmade beige dress
with pin tucks around the collar

I leave the teddy bear in a park
I tell my mom I did it on purpose

untitled 8

it is 2:05 in the morning
your foot on the brake is preventing the car from drifting backwards
he is kissing you first deliberately
then in a lazy or confused way

you know he is trying to communicate something important
and maybe he has wanted you for a long time
but his tongue is moving around your mouth

you begin to wonder if he wants to kiss you
or if he wants to push his way through you

you can see his bedroom window from where you are standing
he is climbing over fences and unlocking them from the inside
he says 'go up those stairs and turn right'

you swear that you would have loved him a year ago
and every day since then

you are waiting at the top of his stairs
you don't know where to look or what to touch
you are thinking about the 'check engine' light in your car

you are aware of certain things while he has sex with you
helicopter noises through an open window
a bottle of blue cough syrup
street signs indicating the direction to an eastbound freeway

he is strong and gentle and you wish he was only one of those things

he is tracing his fingers across the edge of you
everything is quiet other than a barely audible sound
in the space between his arm and his shoulder

he says 'why are you sighing so much'
you say 'that is just how I breathe'
he says 'you don't want to be here'

when I die you can have my heart-shaped sunglasses

I can feel your age
on top of me, looking down at me
sitting next to me and feeling calm
about this massive empty space

they told me that trust versus mistrust
is the primary psychological dilemma of early childhood

I was six years old when I observed you hugging me from a
conceptual distance
only later could I understand the permanency of rejection
'nobody's fault really'

I watched you fall through layers of fabric that day
I watched you speak in unintentional rhyme
and I allowed morbid details
to claim empty space in my head

do you remember that night
when I touched the bottom of the ocean with my tongue
when I felt inadequacy in my spinal column
and valued your quiet existence

now can you understand
a person's hand pushing on my face
and his fingers in my mouth

this is understood to be the defining element of emerging adulthood

induced-compliance paradigm

tomorrow I will call you and tell you
that I have been drunk for a week straight
I want to know what you think about this
because I value your opinion

I enjoy being bitten during sex
because of the causal connection
between the act of biting and
the feeling of being bitten

in the dark I scroll upward for an hour
I read two years worth of text messages

you tell me something
I agree with you

I will ruin everything eventually
I hope this makes sense to you

infinite number of half-distances

you lie on the floor of your room
you bite your fingers until they bleed
you feel something motionless at the base of your head
in the morning you can't feel your arms
nothing to write about, not really
you take drugs alone
and stumble around your house
they tell you that your body is proportioned well
you think they want you, sometimes
you think they will make you better
you can feel anything for a few minutes
nothing leads to improvement
you identify with people who criticize you
at night you think about loving things only a little bit
in the morning, you read about economic collapse
or time moving in a different direction
the edges of things seem abruptly hard to define
you park your car in the dark
become startled and drive somewhere else

this friday I woke up at 2 pm

I started drinking alcohol at 3 pm
at 11 pm I went to a party wearing the same clothes I wore on
thursday
at 12:30 am the guy I lost my virginity to told me he is having a baby
at 1:30 am I ate drugs in the bathroom without telling anyone
I don't know how to maintain relationships
most of the people I've had sex with have negative feelings about me
now
starving to death during sex is something I would like to do this week

here is what I ate today: coffee, curry vegetable thing from whole foods, plum

I am most comfortable around people who criticize me
I feel like anyone who isn't constantly criticizing me is lying
or expecting me to be something different
it feels insane that you need money to do things like
develop a drug addiction, or move across the country
I don't identify as depressed even though I feel depressed
it seems unfair that I only get to feel a finite amount of things in my life
lately I have been assuming that dried fruit has more calories than
regular fruit
I feel like 400 dead jellyfish in the middle of a freeway

2 weeks ago I was looking for drugs at a party

thinking about dying makes me feel tiny and calm
I feel disinterested in dying right now
at 2 pm I took pain killers and walked to the beach
I touched a crab and a sea urchin and a squishy thing
I think I am going to stop wearing my glasses
things seem better when I can't see clearly
I want to have an emotion that feels like being slowly punched in the
face for 3 years

in public places you sit or stand quietly

you try to not draw attention to yourself
you are considerate and polite in social situations
you hide certain opinions and express other ones
you want people to perceive you as agreeable
anyone can enjoy your presence for a short period of time
you allow people to project appealing qualities onto you
for this reason they maintain relationships with you
for a few weeks, months, a year or two
you take drugs because they make you feel different
benzodiazepines make you feel detached, affectionate
as if your opinions and desires exist independently of you
amphetamines make you feel thinner, more sociable
you are equally compelled by experiences with extremely positive or
extremely negative outcomes
physically attractive people don't appeal to you
you feel compelled by people based on their ability to change things
your perception of reality, the ways in which you assign connotation to
memories
you are interested in people who, when thought of years from now,
will cause you to recall certain, specific, crippling emotions

today my alarm went off at 12:30 pm

I stayed in bed for over an hour
looked at things on my phone
I felt slightly anxious about nothing particular
I walked downstairs and poured coffee into a jar
I asked a person on the internet if I should take drugs
I took drugs before the person had time to respond

I feel alienated by people who express concern about me without
defining their concern in terms of a specific solution or goal
I dont feel comforted by the idea of an afterlife
I dont want to continue experiencing things after I die
I want someone to pull my hair because I like the idea of someone
controlling my head without touching my head

what is the difference between being an independent person
and being a person who is accepting of loneliness

today I drove to a house and took care of a baby

I walked the baby to a park
she crawled and waddled around the grass
she picked some flowers and tried to put them in her mouth
she threw slices of bread at birds
I said 'try tearing it into smaller pieces'
she gestured for me to pick her up
while I held her, she put her hand on my right tit
I said 'I cant nurse you, I dont have any milk'
she looked confused then fell asleep immediately
she didn't wake up when I put her in the crib
I turned on the baby monitor and looked at my face in a mirror
I noticed something asymmetrical about my mouth
I wanted to cover my entire body with the world's heaviest blanket

I feel more lonely when I am with people than I do when I am alone looking at the internet

in social situations I hide specific parts of my personality that I think other people might perceive as unappealing
I don't feel like I am pretending to be something different than what I am
I don't feel like I am anything really
I am very tired all the time
I don't identify with most people
I don't think highly of myself
I am too passive to create a situation in which I convince another person that I am valuable
that I am someone who deserves things
that my physical presence in the world should induce positive or negative feelings
everyone is growing apart from me
I am letting them do that

it is 10 am and I am drinking coffee out of a jar

I am parked across the street from a cemetery in a 2 hour parking spot
I will sit here for an hour then pay the meter and sit here for an
additional hour
in my car, things seem okay
outside, a drug deal is happening
I only feel comfortable in enclosed spaces
what's the opposite of claustrophobia
'agoraphobia is an anxiety disorder
characterized by anxiety in situations where
the sufferer percives the environment
to be difficult or embarrassing to escape'
the internet says you can get prescribed xanax for that
everything anyone has ever felt
is a variation of 'sad' or 'happy' or 'angry'
everyone feels the same things over and over again

3.14159265359

you stay alive in your car for three days
then wake up happy and practice alienation

you comfort yourself with the thought
'I am closer to death than I have ever been'

small children extend their arms toward you
desiring something they are unsure about
but know to be reliable
and overwhelmingly vivid

you enjoy being hungry
hunger is a solvable problem

there is a graceless kind of triumph
in every place you have not enjoyed sex

I am going to stop eating

when I am about to die
I will eat four almonds
I want to touch every person in the world at least once
I bought a sandwich then threw it away
I want to snort ambien
does anyone want to do that with me
send me an email

haiku

crying and parking my car
outside a mexican restaurant
a man offered me drugs

1.

I am in the backseat of my car
I am parked on a quiet street

in the shade under a tree
this is where I am most comfortable

2.

I am going to take pain killers
before my ancient philosophy class

I am going to sit in the back
I am not going to say anything

3.

it is 3 o'clock in the morning
you are asleep
I am awake

you snore and I elbow you
you turn over

your hand rests in the narrow part of my waist

4.

if I stop eating food
I will eventually disappear
that is how it works now

5.

today I will send you an email
you will silently acknowledge the email
you won't respond to the email

6.

I want to lie in fetal position on concrete
I think my dentist hates me
I am dipping a tortilla in vodka

7.

what if I exercised every single day
what if I promised to be less shitty

8.

I want to have kids
because what the fuck else am I gonna do

9.

I dont know how to respond to people
who express concern about me

I'm sorry
from now on I will act differently or something

what I think about when I think about the zombie apocalypse

I would kill myself immediately

I wish that you would yell at me and I would yell back and we would both remember that we once had a relationship worth yelling about

it is 2nd grade and the P.E. teacher asks me 'are you feeling alright?'
she says 'why don't you sit with me. would you like me to call your
mom?'
I don't remember if I am crying or not
then I am holding my mom's hand as we walk across black asphalt
my shirt is a comfortable faded green hand-me-down
the weather seems fine because the weather is always fine

I became a bit confused during the year following the death of my
neighbor's cat
there was this vague and permanent yearning for some abstract
emptiness
which manifested in a cold indifference on my fingertips

I touched the sticky dust on the inside of my closet door
and felt guilty about nothing in particular

I intentionally hit my elbow on the corners of tables
and sensed something barely conscious in the wood grain furniture

with a ball point pen, I circled a scar on the base of my left thumb
the necessary emotions for maintaining consciousness
an inability to experience phenomena first-hand

for example: it was christmas day
I wrapped my arms around you from behind
I was sitting cross-legged in the middle of my bed
you were looking down at your phone
I saw you from the perspective of a parallel universe
and your face was infinitely huge

I didn't mind the sex and the car rides
the silent apologies for our inability to create something tangible with
our mouths
I slept so well those nights

mira gonzalez (b. 1992) is from los angeles, california.
she tweets @miragonz.